DISCOVER SERIES
MAMÍFEROS

Búfalo Americano

Oso Pardo

Venado Macho

Alce Toro

Caribú

Coyote

Gama

Bisonte Europeo

Venado Hembra

Zorro

Zorro Cachorro

Toro Gelbvieh

Alce

Cabra de Montaña

Mapache

Huskee Siberiano

Mofeta Rayada

Alce Sueco

Ciervo de Cola Blanca

Jabalí

Alce Amarillo

Hembra Joven

Make Sure to Check Out the Other Discover Series Books from Xist Publishing:

Published in the United States by Xist Publishing
www.xistpublishing.com
PO Box 61593 Irvine, CA 92602

© 2018 by Xist Publishing All rights reserved
Translated by Victor Santana
No portion of this book may be reproduced without express permission of the publisher
All images licensed from Fotolia
First Spanish Edition

ISBN: 978-1-5324-0721-5   eISBN: 978-1-5324-0722-2

Xist Publishing

www.ingramcontent.com/pod-product-compliance
Lightning Source LLC
LaVergne TN
LVHW070951070426
835507LV00030B/3487